# Jojo Leo
# TRAVEL CUTIE
## CUTE & EASY COLORING BOOK

Start your journey by coloring the items every traveler needs. From comfy luggage to trusty travel guides, bring these essentials to life and set the tone for your next adventure! You might even use this coloring book as a fun checklist to get ready for your next big trip.

Thank you for respecting the hard work that went into creating this book!

# WELCOME, COLORING ADVENTURER!

Thank you for choosing this coloring book to celebrate the essentials that make every trip special - from suitcases and travel pillows to passports and maps. These items may be simple, but they're the building blocks of every great journey.

As you color, let each page spark excitement for your next adventure and remind you that the journey begins with the little things. Whether you're traveling far or dreaming from home, I'm glad you're here.

Happy coloring, and may your travels be bright!

With warm wishes,
Your fellow travelers - Jojo and Leo

# LETS STAY CONNECTED

We'd love to see your beautiful creations and be part of your coloring journey! Share your finished pages, behind-the-scenes coloring moments, and creative flair with us on social media. Connect, inspire, and get inspired by other coloring enthusiasts around the world!

- ✤ Tag us: **@jojoleo_coloring**
- ✤ Use the hashtag: **#jojoleo_coloring**
- ✤ Follow us for updates, new releases, and more fun content!

Your support and creativity mean the world to us, and we can't wait to see how you bring these pages to life. Happy coloring!

## PAPER CHOICE

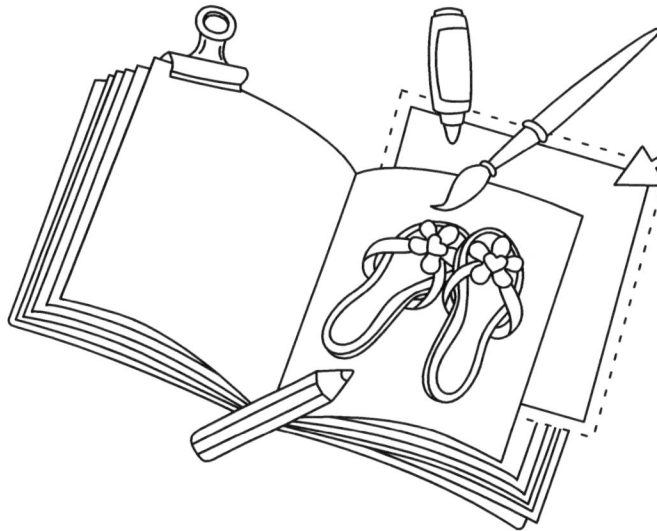

a blank sheet behind the paper to prevent bleeding

Amazon offers a variety of paper options for coloring books, each with its own benefits. We use standard quality paper to keep our books affordable and accessible, and it works best with colored pencils and alcohol-based markers. This choice ensures you can enjoy vibrant, clean results with these mediums while keeping costs reasonable.

If you're using alcohol-based markers, we recommend placing a thicker piece of paper behind the page to prevent bleed-through. Whatever your medium, we hope this book brings your creativity to life!

## WE'D LOVE TO HEAR FROM YOU!

If you enjoyed coloring this book, we'd be so grateful if you could leave a review on Amazon. Your feedback helps us grow and reach more creative minds like yours!

However, if there's anything that didn't meet your expectations, please reach out to us directly. We're always looking to improve and would love the chance to make it right.

Thank you for your support and happy coloring!

## amazon

# A NOTE ABOUT MARKERS AND COLORING PENCILS

## 1 Brush & Fine Tips for Markers:
If you're using alcohol markers, we recommend sticking to the brush and fine tips for the best results. The brush tip is great for smooth gradients and blending, while the fine tip works well for detailed areas.

## 2 Coloring Pencil Tips:
Coloring pencils are perfect for layering and shading. Use light pressure to build up colors gradually, and experiment with blending techniques, like layering similar shades or using a blending pencil.

## 3 Bleed Protection for Markers:
Alcohol markers can sometimes bleed through paper. To protect the next page, place a sheet of cardstock or thick paper beneath the page you're working on.

## 4 Blending & Layering:
Both markers and coloring pencils shine when you layer lightly. Markers are ideal for bold, vibrant colors, while pencils allow for soft, subtle shading. Feel free to mix the two for unique effects!

## 5 Test Your Tools:
Test your markers or pencils on the included Color Test Page (or a blank section of the book) before starting to ensure you're happy with the colors and techniques.

Whether you prefer the bold strokes of markers or the soft touch of coloring pencils, this book is all about having fun and expressing yourself. Enjoy every moment, and happy coloring!

**BRUSH TIP**

**FINE TIP**

**PENCIL**

## THIS BOOK BELONGS TO:

# TEST COLOR PAGE

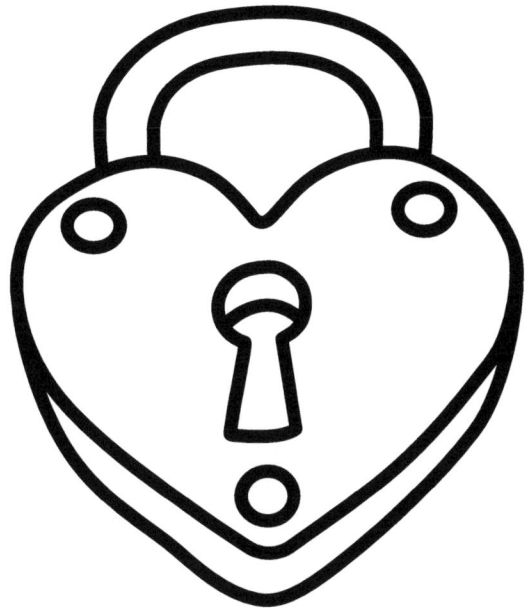

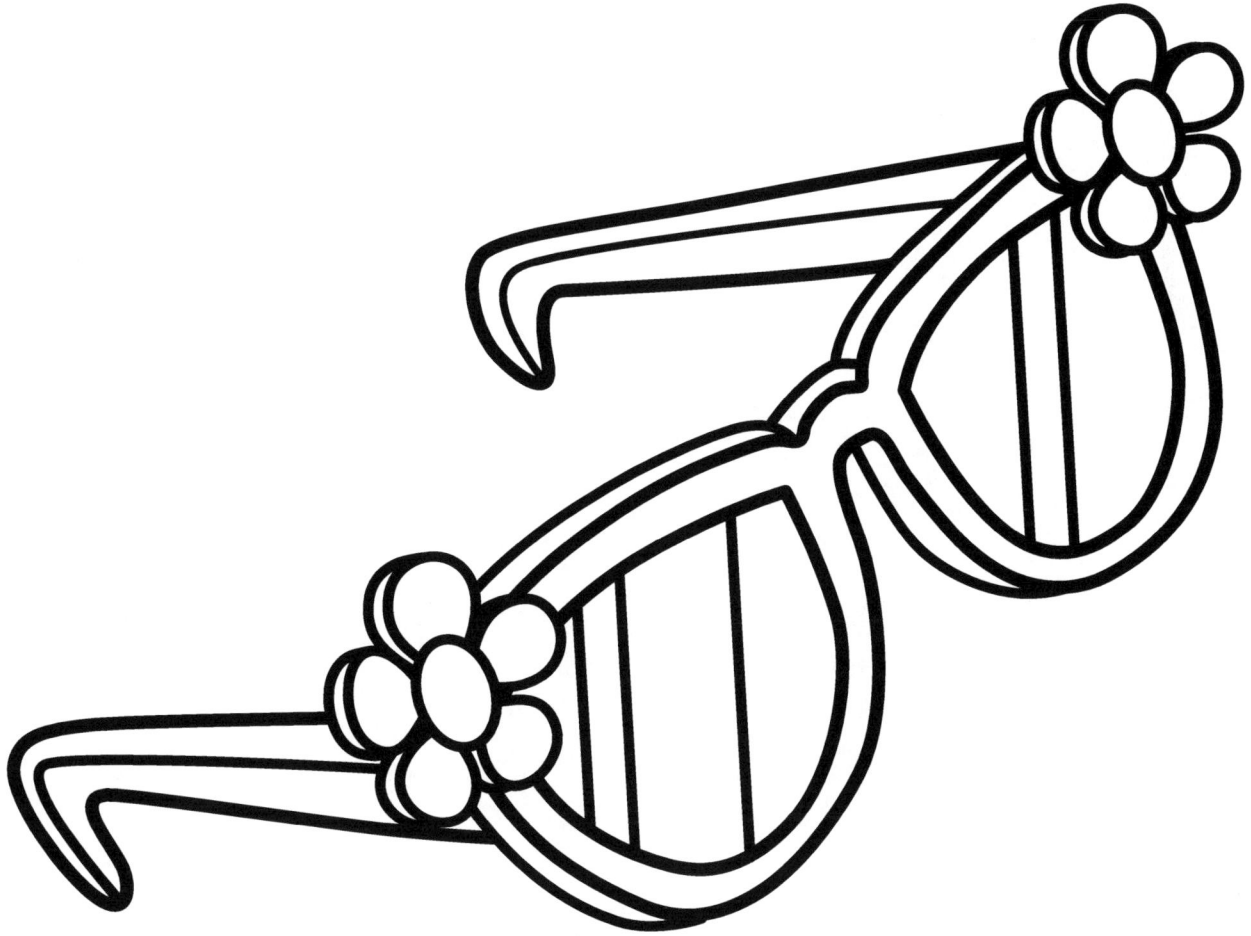

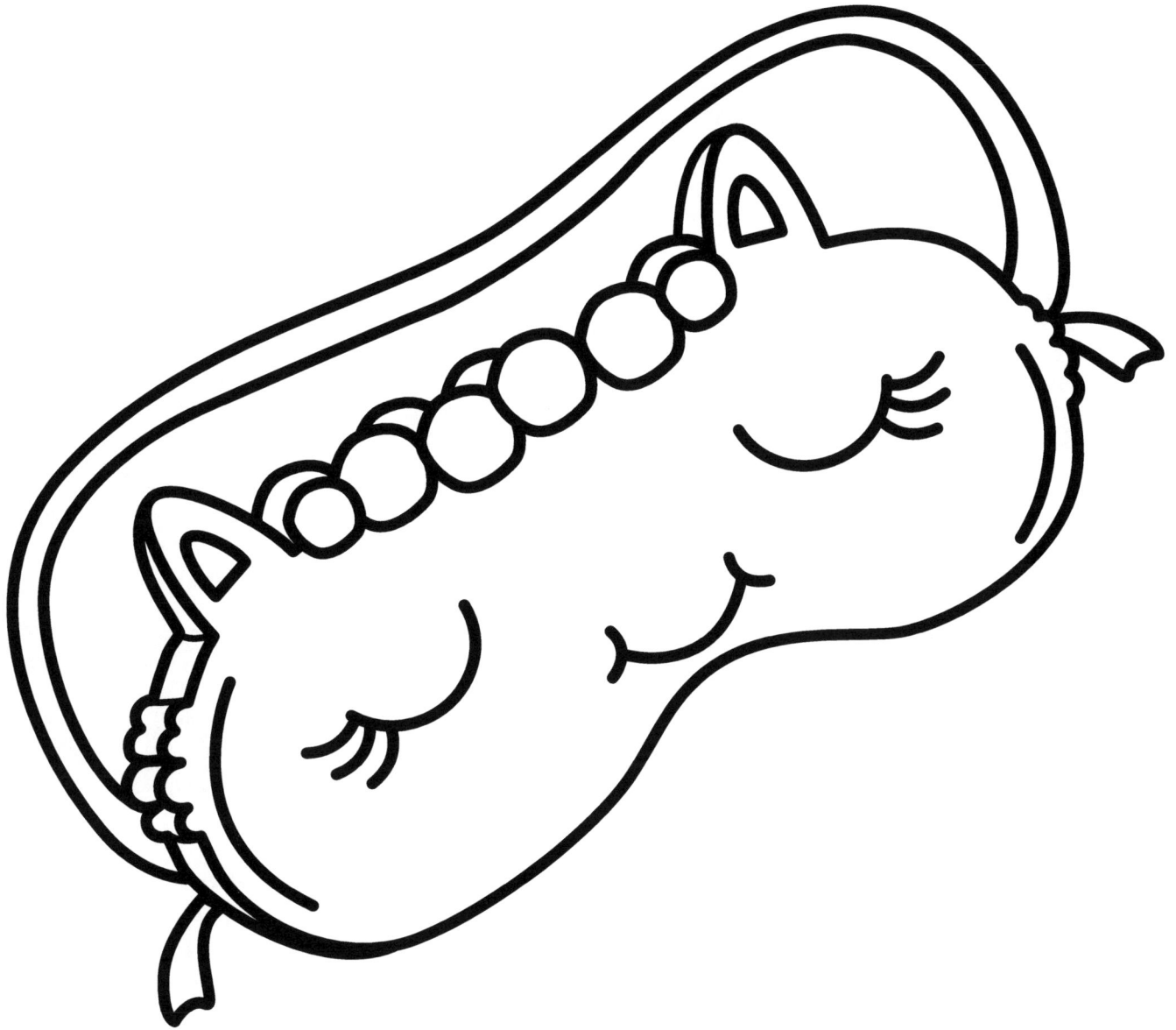

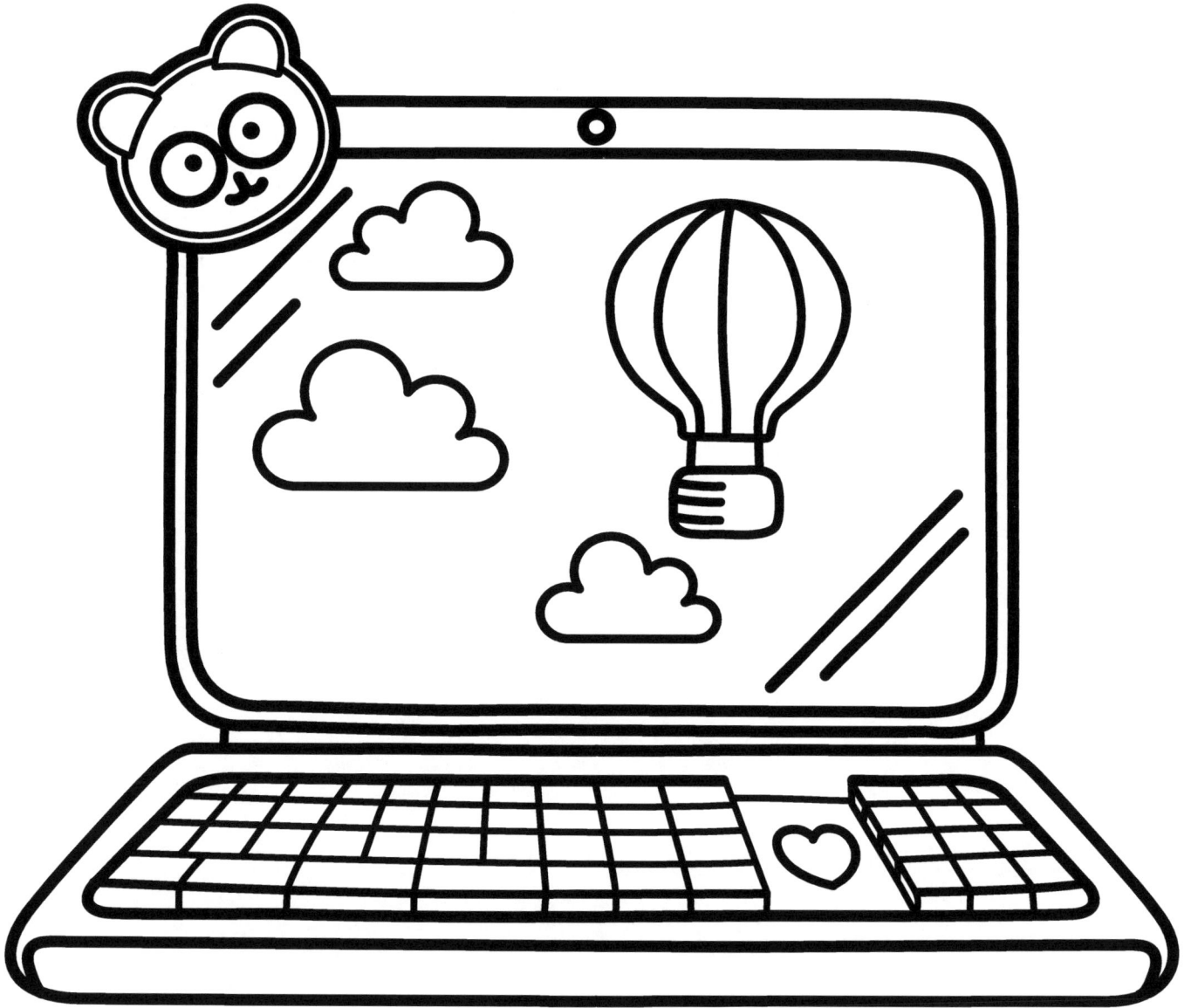

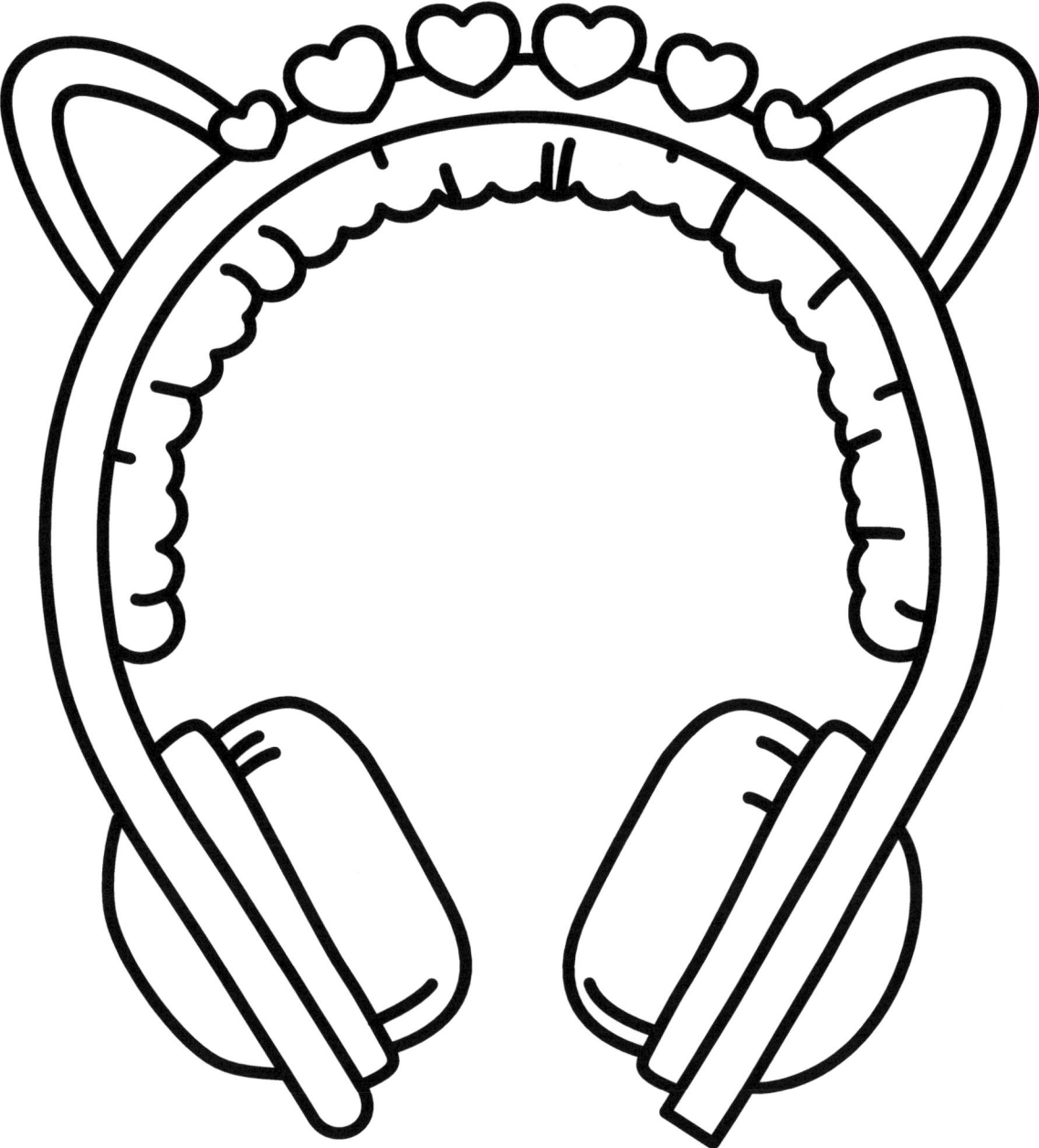

ON THE MOVE

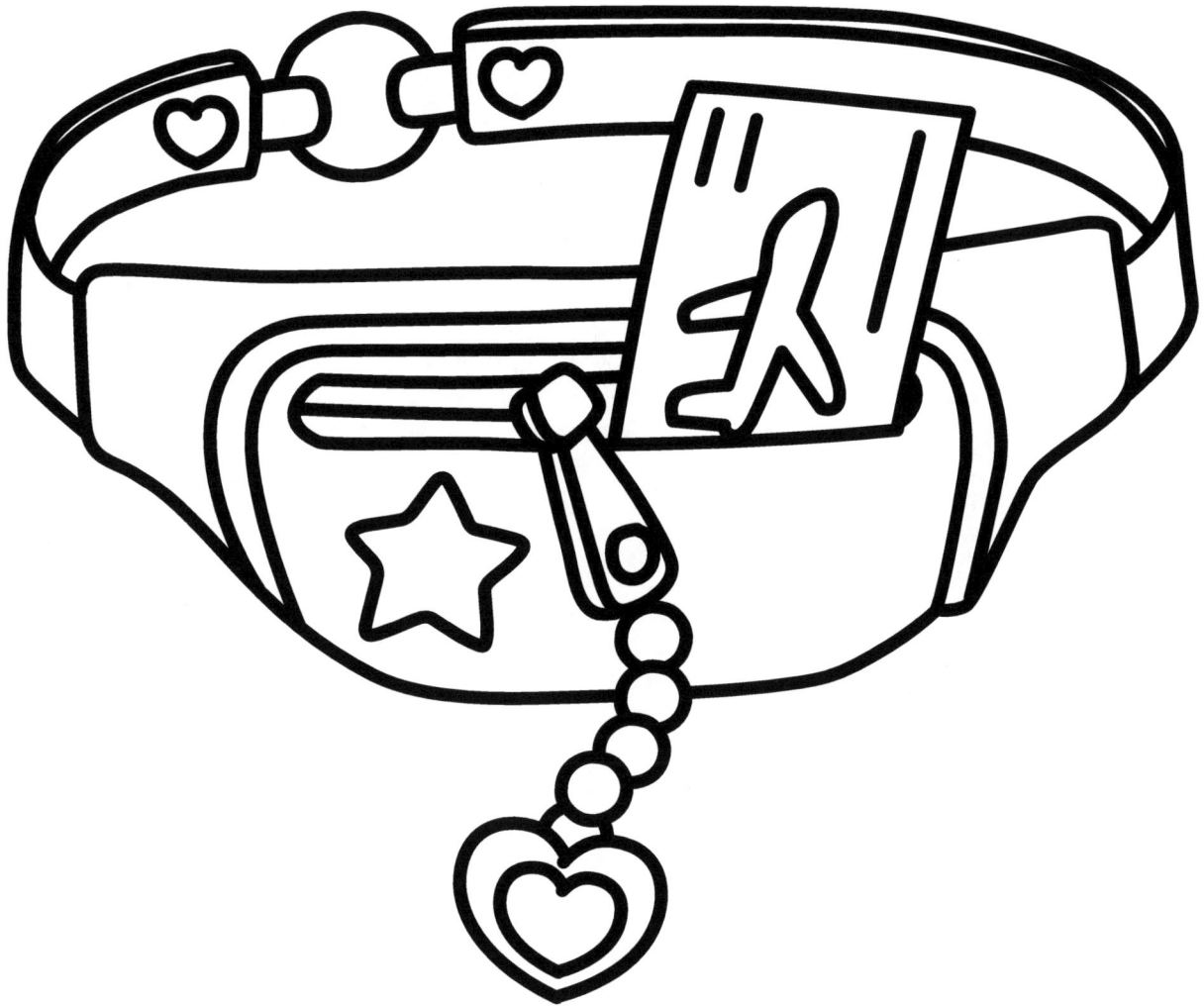

Made in the USA
Columbia, SC
01 July 2025